Mary McLeod Bethune

A Great American Educator

by Patricia C. McKissack

CHILDRENS PRESS ®

CHICAGO

PICTURE ACKNOWLEDGMENTS

Moorland-Spingarn Research Center—Howard University—2, 8, 42, 53 (2 photos), 96
Bethune-Cookman College—22, 50, 51 (2 photos), 52, 54, 55, 62, 80, 88
The Moody Bible Institute—49
Historical Pictures Service, Chicago—56
Cover illustration by Len W. Meents

Library of Congress Cataloging in Publication Data

McKissack, Patricia, 1944-
    Mary McLeod Bethune: a great American educator.

    Includes index.
    Summary: Recounts the life of the black educator, from
her childhood in the cotton fields of South Carolina to her
success as teacher, crusader, and presidential adviser.
    1. Bethune, Mary McLeod, 1875-1955—Juvenile literature.
2. Afro-Americans—Biography—Juvenile literature.
3. Educators—United States—Biography—Juvenile
literature. [1. Bethune, Mary McLeod, 1875-1955.
2. Teachers. 3. Afro-Americans—Biography] I. Title.
E185.97.B34M35   1985   370'.92'4 [B] [92]   85-12843
ISBN 0-516-03218-6

   2 3 4 5 6 7 8 9 10 R 94 93 92 91 90 89 88 87 86

DEDICATION

To Granville and Maxine Sawyer
Thanks Moosies

Table of Contents

To Dan Rathmm
from McLeod Bethum
Mary

Chapter 1

MARY JANE, THE DIFFERENT CHILD

Samuel loved Patsy and wanted to marry her. But he was a slave on the McLeod plantation and she was a slave on the McIntosh place near Mayesville, South Carolina. At first that posed a problem.

Slaves had no control over their lives. They could not even choose their spouses. Decisions involving marriage were usually arranged by the master, and to him it was a matter of economics. Was the woman healthy and able to produce children who would, in time, bring a good price on the slave market? Was the man strong, yet controllable? Runaways were a bad risk. These and other questions had to be settled in the master's mind before he considered a union between slaves. Love had little to do with it.

Why Samuel's and Patsy's masters decided to help them is unknown, but they did agree to an unusual arrangement. Samuel was allowed to purchase his bride with his own labor. Since slaves were not paid wages, Samuel had to use his resourcefulness to earn the money.

Motivated by love, Samuel McLeod worked in the fields from sunup until sundown for no pay. He worked well with tin, leather, and wood, so he had marketable skills. In the evenings he hired himself out to local people for whatever they were willing to pay.

Perhaps the masters believed that Samuel would soon lose interest in a prize so hard to win. Maybe he would forget about Patsy and marry a woman from his own plantation. Another man might have taken this simpler route, but Samuel McLeod was different. He was a stocky man, strong-willed but patient. He knew what he wanted, and love had everything to do with it.

Patsy was different too. She waited for Samuel, knowing that he wasn't going to give up. She was a slave, but never accepted her condition shamefully. No guilt rested on her strong shoulders. Her ancestors were said to have been African nobility, and Patsy took pride in that. For example, she walked erectly and chose not to hide her kinky hair beneath a bandanna. Though uneducated, her language was refined, and she often accentuated her conversations with graceful hand gestures.

In time Patsy and Samuel were married. Soon afterward

their first child, Sallie, was born and thirteen other children followed. Although Patsy was proud and Samuel was industrious, they were still slaves and subject to their master's will. One by one they saw their children sold to other plantations. As soon as one of their sons was able to hold a hoe or chop wood, he was sold. As soon as one of their daughters was able to peel a potato or set a table, she was sold. Samuel and Patsy were powerless to stop it. They only knew about their children from passersby who brought news about them.

But a change was coming. The black McLeods knew little about the movement that was underway. A determined group of people called "abolitionists" were working to change not only their own lives, but the lives of all slaves. If the black McLeods had been able to read, they might have seen the "Wanted" posters offering five thousand dollars for Harriet Tubman. Tubman was a runaway slave who single-handedly led hundreds of her people to freedom on the Underground Railroad. This was not a real train, but a network of anti-slavery people who helped runaways to freedom. Runaways were hidden in barns, attics, and cellars until it was safe to move on to the next "station." In this way, step by step, and with the North Star always in front of them, the slaves moved toward freedom.

Patsy and Samuel couldn't read, but if they could they might have read *Uncle Tom's Cabin*, a novel by Harriet Beecher Stowe. This book was a rallying point around which the abolitionists gathered and mustered support for their cause.

If Patsy and Samuel had been free to come and go as they pleased, they might have gone to hear a fiery speech delivered by Frederick Douglass, preeminent spokesman for black people. A former slave, Douglass spoke with firsthand knowledge about a system that maimed the body and soul of his people. He pleaded passionately for the abolition of slavery, and called for men and women of reason to stand united against such oppression. Douglass won many to his side, but very few black people knew about him or his work at that time.

The slavery debate became so heated by the early 1860s that the country split along the Mason-Dixon Line with two armies poised for battle, each side believing that they were right. The political conflict brought about the Civil War and, eventually, the emancipation of the slaves. Abraham Lincoln, the president of the war-torn country, signed the Emancipation Proclamation in 1863. The McLeods, along with millions of other slaves, were freed.

The war ended, leaving the South a devastated wasteland.

Former slave owners, accustomed to being served, found themselves woefully unprepared to manage their large estates without help. They knew nothing about planting and harvesting crops. On the other hand, the former slaves were educationally and economically unprepared to handle their new status. There were no jobs, no housing, no schools. In truth, ex-slaves and ex-masters needed each other. Had southern leaders chosen to deal fairly with the former slaves, building on the concept that all men are free and equal, growth and prosperity in the South might have come faster. Instead, the leaders created a social and economic system so corrupt and unjust it stifled the growth of the entire region for over a century. In the end, nobody benefited.

During the decade following the war, southern landowners instituted the sharecropping system. This farming method divided blacks and whites into two camps—the haves and the have-nots. Black sharecroppers formed the overwhelming majority of the have-nots, while the white landowners held on to the money, land, and political power. Conditions didn't change much from the old plantation days.

The McLeods were different, however. Patsy continued to work for her former master in exchange for land between Mayesville and Sumter, South Carolina. Samuel, and the sons who were still at home, built a small cabin, and the family used their combined strength to plant their first five acres of cotton.

Then on July 10, 1875, Patsy gave birth to a daughter. The midwife hurried out to the field to tell Samuel that he was a father again. Although this was their fifteenth child, the joy and wonder of a new life still excited him. Besides, this child was different. She was a strong and healthy baby, but more than that, she was their first free-born child. That made her special. Samuel McLeod was a poor, uneducated farmer, but on the day of her birth, he made his daughter wealthy. He gave her hope.

"She is a child of prayer, Samuel," Patsy said to her husband. "I asked the Master [God] to send us a child who would show us the way out. . . . I expected He would bless us with a boy. But, His will be done." Over and over she kept saying, "She is different . . . special!"

Even Grandma Sophia, Patsy's mother, made a prediction about her newest grandchild. "This is a different one," she said. "She'll be great."

The McLeods named their daughter Mary Jane. Although there would be two other children born after her, Mary Jane was the one the family always said was destined to do great things. They weren't wrong. Mary Jane McLeod was different.

Chapter 2

MARY JANE, THE COTTON PICKER

The McLeods' neighbors said Mary Jane was different too. Although "different" is not necessarily a negative term, the neighbors used it to mean "homely." In quiet whispers they discussed Mary Jane's distinctive African features as though they were a curse. It would be a full century later before black Americans accepted their dark skin, kinky hair, full lips, and broad noses as beautiful.

But even then, Patsy instilled in her daughter the feeling that she was beautiful—no more, no less than any other human being. Beauty was measured by other standards in the McLeod household—a loving heart, kind thoughts, and willing hands. So throughout early childhood, Mary Jane was blessed with a healthy body and an equally well-developed self-image.

Old Bush was the family's mule, named so because of his bushy tail. Before she could walk, Mary rode along on the mule's back as he plowed the fields. When she was a little older, Patsy gave Mary the responsibility of caring for the family vegetable garden. She took the job quite seriously, and eagerly attacked the weeds that threatened to smother the young seedlings. Young Mary thrived on praise and did her best to gain her parents' approval—so much so that she was dubbed a "tattle-tale" by her brothers and sisters.

William, one of Mary's older brothers, was the family prankster, and was often scolded for misbehaving. One day William decided to kill one of his mother's chickens and cook it. He invited Mary to join him.

"I'm not going to do it," she said, "and if you do, I'm going to tell." William cooked the chicken and made a terrible mess. Mary helped William clean up, but when Patsy got back to the cabin, just as she had said, Mary told her mother everything. William got a terrible spanking, but it was Mary who cried. "You shouldn't have done it, William," she said. "You knew I was going to tell." William tried to console his little sister. He realized Mary couldn't help but be totally honest. But in the future, William hid his pranks from Mary as much as he did from his mother.

Patsy continued to cook for her former master to help pay for seeds and supplies, and served as the community midwife since there was not a regular doctor in the area. Samuel bought more land with help from his grown sons, and the farm grew from five acres to over fifty acres. They called their farm the "Homestead." It took every available hand to keep the farm running, so every family member was expected to do a share of the work. Only Grandma Sophia, who was too old, was exempt from work.

As soon as Mary was old enough, she was taken to the fields. Cotton plants grow close to the ground, so picking cotton was back-breaking labor. Singing helped to lessen the burden. Playing games, too. One game Mary enjoyed was "Who will spot the first cotton bloom." While working the rows, she kept her eyes sharply peeled for the first sign of a bloom. A treat was in store for the first to spot one. Mary Jane always won, and Samuel rewarded her with a peppermint candy stick.

Later Mary learned that it wasn't just a childish game she was playing. Her father wasn't a scientific farmer who grew according to charts and all their changeable moods. Time was measured by the various stages of the cotton. From the time the first cotton blooms were spotted, he could predict exactly when it was time to pick. From the amount of blooms, he could estimate the success of that year's crop.

Mary came to accept hard work as a virtue. But fun times were no less appreciated. In the evenings the family ate, said prayers, and entertained themselves with lively stories and songs. Often neighbors were invited to share a moment of relaxation in the front yard. But at sunrise everybody went back to the fields. That was the rhythm of Mary Jane's young life, a routine that was interupted only for births and burials.

Religion also played an important part in the McLeod household. The Bible rested on a shelf Samuel built to hold it. Although nobody could read, the family drew comfort from its presence in the house.

There were no churches for black people in Mayesville. A "circuit rider" was a preacher who traveled from one churchless community to the next, delivering his sermon at a designated meeting house. The Homestead was where everyone gathered to worship when the circuit rider came to Mayesville.

Not all of the McLeods' neighbors were black. There were poor white sharecroppers and small farmers who struggled to make ends meet as well. Even though they shared many common problems, there existed an invisible line that neither side was willing or, in those times, even able to cross. This line was drawn early for Mary Jane.

She had a friend named Jennie, a girl about her age. Jennie's family was white, but Mary never considered color a condition of friendship. Jennie frequently ate at the McLeods' house. When Jennie asked Mary to eat with her, Patsy refused to let Mary go. "You would be expected to go around to the back door, and I'm not going to let you do that," said Patsy with unyielding pride. Mary didn't argue the point.

A while later, Jennie was invited to a special event. She confided in Mary that she had nothing decent to wear. Mary Jane let Jennie borrow her best dress and hair ribbons. Whatever her parents may have thought, Jennie wore the dress and returned it in perfect condition. Mary felt vindicated. Whites and blacks could be friends.

Two little girls sharing a dress did not change the general attitude that prevailed among the races. Mary saw the fruits of racial hatred one day on the street. Mary knew both men. The black man had visited her father; she knew his children. The white man had done business with Samuel. "Blow out this match," said the white man after lighting a cigarette. The black man refused. There was a struggle, and the white man ended up on the ground. A mob seized the black man and lynched him. Samuel hurried Mary away from the scene, but the angry mob remained in her mind for as long as she lived.

"Why do they hate us so?" she asked Samuel.

"Because we're colored," he answered.

These and other incidents left a lasting impression on young Mary Jane McLeod. She never forgot them. Though her parents did everything they could to protect her from the harsh realities of the world they lived in, she was rapidly learning the horrible truth. As a black person she was not considered equal.

Never before was that made clearer than the day Mary went with her mother to the "big house" where Patsy continued to cook. Mary Jane was introduced to the girl who lived there, and the two went off to play. After playing with dolls and toys, Mary Jane was drawn to a book sitting on a table. She picked it up and looked at the mysterious squibbles on each page. She pretended that she was reading. Suddenly the white child lashed out. "Put down that book," she said. "You can't read it!"

It was the truth. Mary Jane couldn't read. But why did the truth hurt so much? Why had there been so much anger in the girl's voice? There was something else Mary heard in the angry words—fear. Were white people afraid to let black people read? If so, why? Mary bombarded Patsy with whys.

"You did nothing wrong," Patsy assured her daughter. "You could learn to read if you had the chance."

"Why aren't there any schools for us?"

"Because we're colored," said Patsy. This only gave rise to

other questions for which there never seemed to be satisfactory answers.

Later that night, Mary Jane touched the Bible. "I will read," she said. "God willing, I will read!" From that day on, Mary's mind was preoccupied with the thought of learning to read. When she hoed the cotton, she thought of learning. When she picked the cotton, she thought about reading. Mary Jane McLeod, the cotton picker, raised her hands to the sky. "God," she prayed, "deliver me."

Mary McLeod Bethune, the first free-born child of Samuel and Patsy McLeod, was born in this house in Mayesville, South Carolina. Two of Mary Bethune's nieces pose in front of her birthplace.

Chapter 3

MARY JANE McLEOD, THE READER

Mary finished picking about a hundred pounds of cotton. Her back needed a rest so she lifted her head and wiped the perspiration from her forehead. A strange woman was coming toward her. Mary chuckled to herself. What was a woman dressed in city clothes doing in a cotton field? She hadn't come to work, that was for sure. Samuel went to greet the lady. Seized by curiosity, Mary dropped her sack and hurried over to join them, just in time to hear the lady say, "My name is Miss Emma Wilson, and I've been sent by the Presbyterian Mission Board to start a school for Negro children. I see you have school-aged children," she added, looking at Mary.

Stunned by the reality, Mary looked from Miss Wilson to her father to her mother, then back to Miss Wilson. School! In Mayesville!

"We need all the help we can get here in the fields," Mary

heard her father tell the new teacher. "I'm not so sure we can let our children . . ."

Patsy looked at her daughter's face. "Samuel," she said in her quiet way, "we can spare one set of hands. Mary wants learning more than anything. Let her go."

If anybody could persuade Samuel, it was Patsy. After a moment of thought to convince himself that he was still in charge, he nodded his agreement. "She'll be going to your school," he answered. Miss Wilson turned to Mary and touched her face. "I'll be waiting to see you very soon." Mary McLeod dropped to her knees and raised her hands to the heavens. "Thank you, God," she whispered. "I'm going to learn how to read!"

That evening after the chores were done, Mary took the Bible from its shelf. "I'm going to read this one day," she said. And the family sang happy songs and told stories that livened their hearts.

For the first day of school Samuel bought his daughter a slate board and chalk. Patsy washed and ironed Mary's best dress and hung it up carefully so it would not get wrinkled.

Long before sunrise Mary was up and washed. She could hardly sit still while Patsy combed her hair and tied ribbons on the ends of each pigtail. With a lunch pail under her arm, and cheered by words of encouragement, nine-year-old

Mary Jane McLeod went off to Miss Emma Wilson's school.

The long walk into Mayesville didn't bother Mary. Along the way she daydreamed, then to liven her step she sang one of her favorite spirituals, "Climbing Jacob's Ladder." She pretended that each step was a step up. She was climbing... higher... higher.

Miss Wilson was standing at the door to greet her pupils on that first day. Mary looked around to see who among her friends had been permitted to come. They giggled and admired Miss Wilson, who was about the prettiest lady they had ever seen.

Miss Wilson rang the school bell and fifteen busy little bodies tried to form a straight line. With a gentle smile the teacher ushered her class inside the school. At best the "school" was a makeshift shack with four walls and a roof. There weren't enough desks and very few supplies, but Mary Jane didn't notice these inadequacies. She was out of the fields and inside a school and that's all that mattered.

Of course her brothers and sisters were rather disgusted when she couldn't read after the first day. Patsy chided them, "Reading takes time. She'll learn soon enough." That evening the family gathered around the fireplace and listened to "the different child" recount every detail.

After that first day, Mary McLeod was consumed with

learning. She never missed a day—rain or shine. Her enthusiasm was based as much on respect for Miss Wilson as it was on her love of school. The two really were inseparable in her mind. Mary was thoroughly impressed with Miss Wilson. The child had never met any black people who used "Miss," "Mr.," or "Mrs." before their last name. Those titles were reserved for white men and women. Even her mother, the proud one, was referred to as "Aunt Patsy." Mary liked the sound of *Miss* Mary Jane McLeod, and decided that one day "Miss" was going to be a permanent part of her name. For all her students, Miss Wilson was a living example of what education could help a person achieve. She made an excellent role model.

In a few weeks, Mary Jane learned the alphabet and the sound of each letter. By the end of the first month Mary knew that letters formed words and words contained ideas and information. Words were like the tools of a craftsman, and she was determined to master them so she would never again be told, "Put that book down. You can't read it!"

By the end of the year Mary was able to read. Patsy and Samuel listened with pride as their daughter read from the Bible, recited poetry, and sang. They couldn't help but notice the remarkable change their daughter had undergone physically and mentally. From her mother Mary had inherited graceful hands, which she used expressively when talking. Patsy's mark was on the child in other ways that couldn't be seen on the exterior. Like her mother, Mary Jane had an inner strength, a quiet patience, and limitless energy. She would call on them many times in her lifetime.

From Samuel, Mary inherited a lyrical voice, the capacity to accept hardship with dignity, and the tenacity to see a thing through to the end. Then there were characteristics in Mary that were uniquely her own: her fighting spirit, her inability to accept something wrong because others said it was right, her reverence for life, and her capacity to love. These and other traits surfaced during that first year of school. Samuel gave Patsy a knowing nod whenever Miss Wilson stopped by to give a glowing report of Mary's progress. Their decision to take their daughter out of the fields had been a good one.

The next school year, Miss Wilson returned and the Mission Board built a permanent school and church. Reverend J.C. Simmons was sent as a second teacher, principal, and pastor of the new church. Together he and Miss Wilson expanded the curriculum and recruited more children. Unfortunately, many students from the first year had dropped out, most of them to work the fields. But Mary stayed.

During the second year she was introduced to numbers.

They were as wonderful as words. With only a basic under-standing of math, Mary became aware of how much her people were being cheated at the cotton and rice markets. Uneducated sharecroppers were being routinely taken ad-vantage of, including her father! She was furious.

Sharecropping was a system that made sense in theory but never worked in practice. The standard agreement was simple. A farmer agreed to "rent" land from a large land-owner. There was usually a small shack on the land where the farmer and his family could live. At harvest time the landowner and farmer were supposed to share any profits. In practice something else happened. The landowners kept the records, weighed the harvest, and set the prices. That's when the cheating occurred. The farmer usually ended up owing the landowner after doing all the work, then was told "You ought to work a little harder next year, boy." Those who knew better were afraid to buck the system. People who spoke up very often disappeared.

Even the McLeods, who were landowners, found it diffi-cult to make ends meet because of cheating at the market-place. When his cotton was weighed, Samuel looked at the scales even though he couldn't read them. Somehow, he never had as much cotton as he thought. If only he could read those scales.

Mary secretly decided to do something about the situation. If she told her parents, they wouldn't approve. Mary insisted that she go to the cotton market with Samuel. As usual, the man hoisted the heavy cotton bale on the scale.

"Oh, that's four hundred pounds," he told the farmer. Mary clearly saw that the scale said five hundred pounds. She kept her peace. Samuel was next.

"Oh look," shouted Mary before the man could speak. "We've got six hundred pounds of cotton." The man was astonished.

"Right smart little girl you got there," he said. Samuel smiled. For the first time, Samuel was paid full price for his cotton, and managed to make a small profit.

What Mary had done was potentially dangerous. If the man had thought she was trying to confront him, he might have reacted differently. But Mary was learning a very valuable lesson—how to use her education tactfully, to avoid confrontation.

When the neighbors, both black and white, learned that Mary could write and "figure" numbers, they came to the cabin and asked her to help them figure their bills, read papers, and write letters. She did so willingly.

For four years Mary attended Miss Wilson's school. On graduation day, Mary proudly accepted her certificate along with a handful of other students who had endured. The students presented a program that included singing and poetry reading, with statements of encouragement from Reverend Simmons and Miss Wilson.

Back at the Homestead the celebration continued, but Mary's thoughts were elsewhere. "What now?" she asked herself. Was she expected to go back into the fields after four years of school? There was so much more to know. She confided in Miss Wilson.

"There is a school in Concord, North Carolina," said her teacher and mentor. "But, it's costly. I'll speak to your father."

Samuel didn't need Patsy's coaxing this time. "I'll make the sacrifice," he said. "I'll pay for her to go to that school somehow." Patsy nodded her approval.

Miss Wilson made the arrangements. Mary was going to Scotia Seminary in the fall. Once again she remembered to thank her God.

Then Old Bush died. One morning the old mule was pulling the plow. Suddenly he stopped; his body jerked, then he fell over. After a close inspection, Samuel announced, "Mule's dead." When they buried the faithful old mule at the end of the field, Mary threw her "going-to-school dreams" in the hole with him. She wept as Samuel covered them with dirt.

Mary's tears were as much for herself as they were for Old Bush. School was now out of the question. She was mature enough to know the family had to buy another mule, but still the child mourned for her lost dream.

Mary prayed silently and asked for guidance. Always she added, "God, Your will be done." And miraculously, help did come. Miss Wilson came to the house, out of breath with excitement. "Mary, you've been awarded a scholarship. You're going to Scotia after all."

When Miss Wilson explained the whole story, the family joyfully gave thanks.

"It's a miracle," said Mary.

Indeed it was a miracle. A dressmaker in Denver, Colorado, named Mary Crissman (sometimes spelled Chrissman) offered her life savings as a scholarship to one black child. Mary had been selected based on Miss Wilson's recommendations, Mary's personal achievement, and her desire for higher education.

Later in life Mary McLeod said of Miss Crissman:

> Oh, the joy of that glorious morning! I can
> never forget it. To this day my heart thrills
> with gratitude at the memory of that day. I was
> but a little girl, groping for the light, dreaming

dreams and seeing visions in the cotton and
rice fields and away off in Denver, Colorado, a
poor dressmaker, sewing for her daily bread,
heard my call and came to my assistance. Out
of her scanty earnings she invested in a life—
my life!

Word spread quickly: "Sam's daughter is going off to
school."

Although it meant Mary would have to leave her family,
her parents agreed, once again, that they were doing the
right thing.

The day Mary Jane McLeod left Mayesville, all work
stopped. Her neighbors turned out in full force to give one of
their own a proper send-off. Some brought presents, and
others who had nothing to give, gave their best wishes. After
a tearful good-bye Mary boarded the train. Someone started
a chorus of "We Are Climbing Jacob's Ladder," just as the
train pulled slowly away. Little Mary, the cotton picker,
who had walked five miles to learn how to read, was on her
way, higher . . . higher.

Chapter 4

MARY JANE McLEOD, THE STUDENT

When Mary McLeod entered Scotia Seminary in 1887 she was twelve years old. She would not return home until she was nineteen.

Mary was met at the station by Mrs. Satterfield, the principal's wife. The woman had kind eyes, and Mary felt comfortable with her. During the short buggy ride, Mary became more and more apprehensive. Where was she going and what was it going to be like? She had never in her wildest imaginings dreamed of a place like Scotia.

They stopped in front of Graves Hall, a three-story colonial building with large white pillars. *This* was to be her new home? It was larger than the big house where Patsy worked. As Mary stepped into the large entry hall her eyes were fixed on the winding staircase with its polished banister. Still awestruck, she followed Mrs. Satterfield to her room on the third floor.

Although Mrs. Satterfield was telling Mary where she could find this and that and pointing out interesting features in the great mansion, Mary didn't hear a thing. She stood in the middle of the floor, trying to still her heart.

"This is Abbie Greely, your roommate," said Mrs. Satterfield. Abbie smiled and welcomed Mary to her room at Scotia. "Show Mary where to put her things, and I'll see you at dinner." Mrs Satterfield left quietly—only the soft rustle of her skirt could be heard.

One look at Abbie made Mary want to run to Mrs. Satterfield and beg to be sent home. Abbie was everything Mary wanted to be, but knew she wasn't—not then at least.

Mary went to the window and looked out over Scotia grounds. Flowers were growing instead of vegetables. As far as she could see there was green grass, but no fields. Nothing but trees and shrubs, flowers and woods everywhere. She had never seen so much unplowed land in her life. Everything was different. Even her bed was soft, not scratchy like her straw-filled mattress at home.

Abbie told Mary she was from Greensboro, North Carolina. The older girl explained briefly what Scotia was like. "You'll learn to love it. Come on, now, freshen up. Dinner is at six sharp!"

Nervously, Mary entered the dining room.

A crystal chandelier hung from the ceiling. Paintings decorated the walls, and vases of freshly-cut flowers sat on highly-polished furniture. The table was set with a tablecloth, matching napkins, and a full set of silverware. Then came the shock of her life. White and black teachers were served at the same table. It was all too much for a poor farmer's daughter. Her appetite vanished and a lump settled in her stomach. Everyone seemed to understand, and Mrs. Satterfield excused Mary. Mary never felt so out of place. How could she ever fit in? But as much as she wanted to, she didn't go home.

Mary had no way of knowing then, but all the girls who came to Scotia were just as frightened and unsure of themselves as she was. Even Abbie. Even most of the teachers.

Although she was stunned at first, Mary quickly adjusted to her new environment. Once she learned more about where she was and the people who surrounded her, she relaxed. She learned that Scotia Seminary was founded in 1867 by the Presbyterian church to educate black children. In the beginning all the teachers had been white, with Dr. David J. Satterfield serving as principal. The school was equivalent to our present-day high school and junior college combined. Many of the black teachers were former students.

During the seven-year course of study, Mary was introduced to math, science, English, social studies, Latin, home economics, and religion. She managed to make good grades in spite of her heavy work schedule. Mrs. Crissman's scholarship didn't cover all the tuition, so Mary had to work to meet expenses. She didn't mind, because at Scotia even work was a learning experience. While working in the kitchen she learned about nutrition and how to prepare food in new and exciting ways. While dusting she took time to study the paintings. Gardening introduced her to flowers and vegetables she had never seen.

During her free time, Mary wrote letters to her family back home. Miss Wilson read them to Mary's parents and wrote back with all the local news. Mostly Mary read, and read, and read. She was searching for her life's work. More and more she was determined that she wanted to be of service to mankind. A teacher? A missionary, perhaps? She liked that idea. Once she heard a preacher talk about Africa. She fancied she heard the voices of her ancestors calling to her. A missionary in Africa! That seemed a worthy career. It was settled. She wrote to Miss Wilson about her decision.

Mary's constant push for learning might have led some to believe she was all work and no play. Quite the contrary. Mary McLeod was a fun-loving, happy person who knew how to laugh at herself.

Biddle University in Charlotte, North Carolina, was an all-boys school. Each spring Scotia and Biddle came together for two socials. Mary loved to dance and was usually the first to start up a square dance. She was also a terrible flirt.

Storytelling was another way Mary charmed her friends. She delighted the faculty and her classmates with stories, using her deep voice and expressive hands to dramatize each tale. She won many friends with her quick wit and disarming smile.

When new girls came to Scotia, Mary greeted them with kind understanding. She never forgot her first day at Scotia. When she saw the forlorn look in a newcomer's eyes, she teased them or hugged them, whichever seemed most fitting. Some girls could not make the adjustment and returned home. Some had to leave because of illness in the family, lack of money, or just plain homesickness.

Whenever Mary felt lonely, she remembered her goals and the feeling passed. At those times she also treated herself to a piece of peppermint candy, a treat she loved.

Although Dr. Satterfield was known for being strict, he and Mary became good friends. She often visited him in his study and talked about her plans to become a missionary in Africa. Since her stay at Scotia was coming to an end, he encouraged her to apply to Moody Bible College in Chicago. Her letter of application is a matter of record.

Scotia Seminary
Concord, N.C.
May 26th, 1894

Miss L.L. Sherman:
It is my greatest desire to enter your Institute for the purpose of receiving Biblical training in order that I may be fully prepared for the great work which I trust I may be called to do in dark Africa. To be an earnest missionary is the ambition of my life. I was born in Mayesville, South Carolina, July 10th, 1875. My educational advantages were very limited until I came to Scotia Seminary in 1887. I have been here since then and hope to graduate in the Scientific Course here July 13, 1894. My health has been, and is, very good. I shall hope to be able to enter the Institute sometime in July and take the course necessary for my work.

Very truly yours,
Mary J. McLeod

Feeling satisfied that she had done the right thing, she popped a piece of peppermint into her mouth, leaned back in her chair, and kicked up her heels.

Patsy and Samuel were unable to attend their daughter's graduation exercises; they had no extra money. But Mary knew they were proud. Mrs. Crissman shared their pride. Mary's kindly benefactor sent a Bible as a graduation gift, and confirmed that she would continue the scholarship to Moody.

From Scotia Mary went straight to Moody. Moody Bible College was founded by Dwight L. Moody, an evangelist. Wherever he went crowds gathered to hear him speak. Students applied to study at the institute, but the screening process was rigid. Mary felt fortunate to be a student at Moody and became, once again, a willing learner.

"There were no feelings of race at Moody," she said years later. It was not an empty claim. Mary's roommate was white, and that was unheard-of even in the most liberal northern cities.

It was at Moody that Mary developed her musical ability. Her rich contralto voice impressed Dr. Charles Alexander and Dr. D.B. Towner, her musical directors. They strongly suggested that she consider performing on stage. Mary graciously declined. Her mind was made up; she was going to

Africa. However, she enjoyed singing in the choir.

On Wednesdays the Moody singers performed for prisoners. Mary also ventured into the slums of Chicago to evangelize. There she faced rejection but seemed to be strengthened by it. She promised herself that the next time she would try harder, prepare better, change her approach, and be more convincing.

Then in the middle of her final work at Moody, she got word that the Homestead had burned. Samuel mortgaged the farm to rebuild. Mary wanted to help, but she had no money to send them. "My life is one series of miracles," Mary McLeod once told an audience, and she went on to tell this story.

A group of society ladies invited her to perform at one of their seasonal functions. Mary agreed, never thinking she'd be paid. After the program, she was given an envelope that she tucked in her purse. Back at the dormitory she opened the envelope, expecting to find a letter of thanks. The letter was there, but so was a check for $40. At that time, $40 was a considerable amount of money. She sent the money to her parents right away. "God's wonders never cease," Mary McLeod often said.

Mary's year ended at Moody. For many years she had been exposed to wonderful teachers who had prepared her well.

It was time to move on, but not in the direction she had planned.

"There are no openings in Africa for a Negro missionary," she was told. "I was crushed," she said later. "Heartsick. I wanted to go to Africa to save souls, not realizing how much I was needed here." Sometimes it is hard to see the forest for the trees.

Somehow Mary Bethune was able to raise money for her projects.

Chapter 5

"MISS" MARY JANE McLEOD, THE TEACHER

Mary had accomplished much in a short time. Why did she feel so depressed? The train ride from Chicago to Mayesville seemed endless. Mary tried to think cheerful thoughts, but disappointment is a powerful emotion; it can't be so easily dismissed. Going to Africa had meant so much to her.

The train stopped in Mayesville and young Mary stepped off. A neighbor who didn't recognize her asked if he could help. "And who might you be?" the man asked.

"I'm Mary Jane McLeod," she answered.

The man slapped his thigh with a dusty hat. "I do say!" he shouted. "Sam's daughter done come home! I'll be right proud to take you home."

Mary's neighbors didn't allow her to feel depressed too long. Within a few days she was in Miss Wilson's school teaching. "Class, this is Miss Mary Jane McLeod," Miss Wilson said. Mary only heard the *Miss*. How wonderful to be called "Miss." That was a dream come true. Then as she thought, Mary realized that just a few years ago, she had been a cotton picker unable to read or write. She had wanted so badly to read; now she could read. She had wanted to go to Scotia; a way had been provided. She had wanted to go to Moody; she had done that, too. Mary Jane McLeod suddenly realized, standing there in that classroom, that she had no real reason to feel bad.

Miss McLeod worked in Miss Wilson's school for a year, then transferred to Haines Normal Institute in Augusta, Georgia. Miss Lucy Laney, the founder, was a delightful woman who taught Mary the practical side of running a school. Miss Lucy, as everyone called her, never threw away a thing that could be recycled into something else. She used every opportunity to advance her school, and would stand shamelessly on a corner and beg if it meant keeping Haines's doors open. Mary admired Miss Lucy and the two worked well together, each woman respecting the other's abilities. The older woman understood the younger woman's disappointment about Africa. "You're needed here," Miss Lucy told Mary.

After that first year at Haines, Mary never thought about Africa again. She became a missionary in her own country.

Besides, Mary had come to love teaching; it came naturally. She accepted the directorship of the choir, and took the children to sing at churches, private homes—anywhere they were invited. The small donations they collected went to buy food and supplies for the school.

Although Mary did not make a large salary, she sent most of it home to Samuel and Patsy. During that first year Mary bought her parents a house just outside of Sumter, South Carolina. The house had running water, plastered walls, a fireplace, a nice yard, and a porch. Hattie, Mary's baby sister, took care of their aging parents.

At the end of the year, Mary learned that she was being transferred by the mission board to Kindrell Institute in Sumter. That was perfect, she thought. Patsy and Samuel were getting old, and Mary wanted to be near them.

Working at Kindrell was much the same as working at Haines. Mary threw herself into the work and put in more hours than were required.

Estella Roberts, a friend of Mary's, decided to become Mary's matchmaker.

"You never take time for yourself," said Estella. "You're too young to be so sanctimonious!"

Mary looked at herself in the mirror. It was true. For the past two years all she had thought about was teaching. Perhaps Estella was right. She did need other interests.

Mary was young, so it wasn't hard to find a boyfriend. But most of the young men she met were boring. Their conversations were limited and so were their minds. Dating seemed such a waste of time.

"You just must meet this young man named Bethune," said Estella. "He's tall and very handsome—just perfect for you."

Mary refused. "He'll be like all the rest. No thank you. I have better things to do with my time."

"Okay, Mary. If you keep up, you'll be a teacher all your life."

That idea didn't seem so bad to Mary. But Estella would not take no for an answer, so Mary finally agreed to meet the young man.

"Mary, this is Albertus Bethune." Albertus was hopelessly in love after the first date, but Mary claimed she was only slightly interested. However, she agreed to see him again, and everybody who knew Mary knew she was falling in love too.

Albertus had attended Avery Institute in Charleston, but he hadn't gone to college. He was working in a men's clothing store, and supporting his younger brother who was in college. He was soft-spoken and usually chose to be the listener rather than the speaker.

The two spent every spare moment together. Albertus taught Mary how to ride a bicycle and Mary introduced him to music. His tenor voice complemented her contralto.

Everyone knew it was serious when Mary took Albertus to see Patsy and Samuel. After dinner Samuel and Albertus went out on the porch. Patsy and Mary cleared the table and talked about when Patsy had married Samuel. "A slave buying a slave," Patsy laughed. "Now wasn't that something?"

Mary's mother had been very strict with her girls, often warning, "Keep your feet on the ground and your skirt down." Patsy was proud to boast that none of her daughters had married "because they had to." Mary wanted her parents' approval, and they gave it. Samuel and Patsy liked Albertus and gave the couple their blessings.

During Mary's second year at Sumter, in 1898, she and Albertus were married by Reverend J.C. Watkins. From then on she called herself "Mrs. Mary McLeod Bethune." She dropped the "Jane" and kept the "McLeod" to honor her father. His name, through her, would be honored by many.

Albertus accepted a teaching assignment in Savannah, Georgia. (At that time a college degree was not required to teach.) The Bethunes set up housekeeping in a small apartment in the home of Mrs. Ella Lee on Robert Street. It was cozy and comfortable, and Mary enjoyed fixing it up. Within a year Mary learned she was going to be a mother. Mrs. Bethune's teaching career was temporarily put on hold.

Moody Bible students, including Mary Bethune, traveled around Chicago in "gospel wagons" visiting hospitals and jails, and holding Sunday school classes and tent meetings.

Mrs. Bethune and her staff and students pose on the steps of Faith Hall. The school was now coeducational.

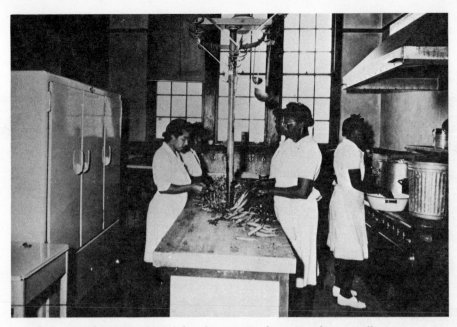

Above: Cooking was one of the classes at Bethune-Cookman College.
Below: A science exhibit prepared by the Bethune-Cookman students in 1928.

In the late 1930s, Keyser Laboratory School, a part of
Bethune-Cookman College, held agricultural classes.

Mary Bethune was very active in civil rights issues. She was very effective as a speaker (above) and also manned picket lines (left) to help the oppressed.

Mary Bethune (center, front row) and members of
the National Council of Negro Women

Mary Bethune and her administrative secretary leaving the offices of the National Council of Negro Women in Washington, D.C.

A 1944 photo of Walter White, head of the NAACP, Mary McLeod Bethune, president of the National Council of Negro Women, and Dr. Channing H. Tobias, field secretary for negro work in the YMCA

Chapter 6

MARY McLEOD BETHUNE, THE DREAMER

Great achievers are usually dreamers. Mary McLeod Bethune was no exception. The unprecedented achievements accomplished in her lifetime began with a vision—a dream. But no one knew better than Mary how quickly a dream can fade unless the dreamer gives it form and substance in the real world. Those who knew Mrs. Bethune best have said that as soon as an idea took shape in her head, she immediately went to work on it, devoting long hours on the project until it was completed.

In the last years of the nineteenth century, Mary was not so sure of herself. She was a new wife and mother, and tradition dictated that she should settle down and tend to her family's needs. She tried to conform, but it didn't work.

Albert McLeod Bethune, "Bert," was born in 1899, the ninetieth grandchild of Patsy and Samuel. When Bert was nine months old, Mary announced she was going to Palatka,

Florida, to teach at the mission school there. She had learned about Palatka from Reverend Eugene Uggans, pastor of the church at Palatka. He had come to Savannah to visit Irene Smallwood, a friend of the Bethunes. After dinner they had discussed the possibility that the four of them might pool their resources to build a school. Reverend Uggans was certain that with the proper leadership the Palatka school could grow. It seemed to him that Mary was right for the job. To the others, it made good after-dinner conversation, but was not a job for Mary.

For some time Mary had been having dreams. The first dream was quite vivid. She saw herself standing by a river with Samuel, Patsy, and Dr. Satterfield from Scotia beside her. They waded into deep water. Soon her father had to turn back. "I can't go with you," he said. Next Patsy turned back. "I can't go where you're going," she said. Then Dr. Satterfield turned back. "You must go on alone," he said. Mary saw herself facing deep, dark waters. She didn't know where she was going, but she had to cross the river alone. She awoke.

Since childhood Mary had had dreams. The midwife who attended her birth predicted she would be a visionary. Mary believed that divine guidance often came in dreams, so she never took them lightly and pondered over the meaning of each one. The message in her first dream was easy to interpret. The people who had supported her the most couldn't help her in the future. Crossing life's river would be difficult, but she could make it. She had been prepared to do so.

In pursuit of that dream, Mary accepted the position in Palatka. Albertus did not share his wife's enthusiasm for teaching; he wanted to be a businessman. Mrs. Bethune went on alone. However, within the year, Albertus realized his wife was never going to be like other wives, so he joined her and they rented a small cottage. From 1899 to 1903 Mary McLeod Bethune helped build the mission school in Palatka, but it was not totally satisfying for her. She still had dreams of starting her own school.

During the winter of 1903, Mary became ill with a fever. For several days she slept fitfully, and another dream came. It was as prophetic as the first. This time she stood on the bank of another river. Behind her were thousands of people asking for help. She couldn't see who they were, or understand how she was to help them, but it was clear that they needed her. Then a man handed her a notebook and said, "You must write down the names of all those you see."

When Mary woke her pastor was sitting beside the bed. She told him the dream. "What does it mean?" she asked. His interpretation was this: "You will build a school. Many young people will pass through your hands, and you will be given a long life to accomplish this goal." Mary McLeod Bethune had much to think about during her recovery.

The fulfillment of that prophecy was nearer than anybody could have imagined. From a friend Mary heard about Daytona, Florida. Blacks had been hired to lay the tracks for the Florida East Coast Railroad. From all reports there were no schools for the black children, and living conditions were inhumane. Disease was widespread among the workers, and children were growing up like animals, taught to steal food to survive. "That's where I am needed," Mary said to Albertus. And, though he protested, she and Bert boarded a train for Daytona.

Everything Mary had been told was true, only it was much worse. With $1.50 in her purse, Mary McLeod Bethune made plans to start a school as soon as possible. But first things first. She had to find a place to stay. Through a mutual friend, she found Mrs. Susie Warren, who welcomed Mary and Bert to her home. The two women liked each other immediately, and Bert enjoyed playing with the young Warren girls.

Then came another dream. Once again, Mary saw herself standing at a river crossing. The river was wide and swift. Crossing the river was like trying to start a school with no money. While she stood contemplating the problem, a man rode up on a beautiful white horse. "Why are you standing here?" he asked. "I am thinking about how I can start my school," Mary answered. The horseman replied, "I am Booker T. Washington." From his coat the great black educator took a handkerchief, wet with perspiration, and wiped his brow. Then he handed Mrs. Bethune a huge diamond. "This will help you build your school." The dream ended. Mary McLeod Bethune never doubted herself or her ability to get the job done again.

Mary Bethune visiting a school north of Daytona Beach, Florida in 1918

Chapter 7

MARY McLEOD BETHUNE, THE BUILDER

Blacks entered the twentieth century with very little hope. Although there had been a few notable personal achievements, the vast majority of blacks were undereducated, overworked, and underpaid. There wasn't much tangible evidence that things were going to change. Mary McLeod Bethune was only one woman, but she was the bearer of hope. She could not fail.

With Mrs. Warren's help, Mrs. Bethune met Mr. John Williams, one of the few black property owners in Daytona. He was a carpenter who had a cottage for rent on Oak Street. Mary Bethune went to see the place. There were three rooms downstairs and two upstairs. Although the house was a mess, Mrs. Bethune knew it had possibilities. The first floor would serve as her school; she and Bert would live upstairs. "I'll take it," she said, agreeing to $11 a month rent. At that moment she didn't have a dime, although she had the money by the time the first month's rent was due.

Slowly the place began to take on the look of a school. When she wasn't cleaning, Mrs. Bethune went to her neighbors and told them her plans. Her enthusiasm was infectious and people willingly donated both time and money. She was a spark of hope in a depressed environment.

Daytona was a typical southern town, divided into two separate unequal communities. The railroad tracks served as the dividing line. Blacks were allowed to cross over into the white section to work, but at sundown they were expected, and enforced by law, to return to "Colored Town."

In order to start her school, Mrs. Bethune needed money. White people had money, so she went to them in their own territory. She refused to be intimidated, and often said, "Ask not, get not." She simply ignored the social barriers, dismissing them as mere barriers of the mind.

Daytona was growing rapidly. In a short while it had become the winter home of America's elite. Mrs. Bethune soon learned that northern businessmen and their wives were generous givers. She approached them with her idea of starting a school, and more often than not, she was given a dollar or two without pause. She accepted donations with gratitude, very often following up with a thank-you note.

On October 3, 1904, Mary McLeod Bethune opened Daytona Educational and Industrial School for Negro Girls in the little cottage on Oak Street. Five girls, ages eight to twelve, came to her that first day. As Miss Wilson had done so long ago, Mary greeted her students with a smile. Her desk was an old packing box. The children used charcoal for pencils and boiled berries to make ink.

Although tuition was fifty cents a week, it didn't cover half the expenses. During the first year it was not uncommon to see Mrs. Bethune rummaging through trash heaps searching for things she could reuse. They baked sweet potato pies and sold them for a quarter. Those first five girls formed a choir. They dressed neatly in uniforms, white blouses and dark skirts. Mrs. Bethune took them to sing in hotel lobbies across the tracks. She taught her girls to graciously accept the small donations after each performance.

There were times during those early days when Mary Bethune would feed the children breakfast, not knowing where dinner would come from. One evening she went to the grocery store. "No more credit, Mrs. Bethune. I must have a payment." That meant the children would have no supper. On the way home she prayed.

A man passed her. "Aren't you Mrs. Bethune, the lady that's started that school for little colored girls?

"I am," she answered.

"I just want you to know I like what you're doing." He gave her $5.00 and continued on his way. Mrs. Bethune hurried back to the store, paid the bill, and bought enough groceries to last a week. "It is by faith that I have come thus far," she said. "My faith will take me on."

Mary McLeod Bethune's reputation as a fund-raiser preceded her. "If she get's you cornered, you might as well reach for your pocketbook," said one sponsor. Mrs. Bethune was her school's only, and later its best, spokesperson. She understood what she was trying to do and knew how to get others to share it with her. All but Albertus. Although he joined her in Daytona and did whatever he could to help, he had his own agenda, and it didn't include starting a school. After a while Mary and Albertus drifted apart.

By 1905 Mrs. Bethune had one hundred students. Although some of them went home in the evening, more and more were live-in students. No child was ever turned away, so larger quarters were necessary.

Without a moment's hesitation, Mrs. Bethune approached Mr. Johnson, her landlord. "I'd like to buy a piece of property from you," she said. "I'm thinking about expanding." After she'd looked at several sites, none of which satisfied her, they passed a trash dump. "That's where my school will be," she said.

Mr. Johnson tried to dissuade her, but once Mrs. Bethune made up her mind, that was it. Mr. Johnson agreed to sell the land for $250—a small down payment and the rest in small monthly payments.

"I'll be back within a few days with your down payment," said Mrs. Bethune.

She didn't have a dime. That was Wednesday. By the following Tuesday, she delivered the $15 down payment—pennies, nickels, and dimes wrapped in a handkerchief. Somehow, she had raised the money. Then she found workers to clear the land, although she had no money to pay them either. Somehow she raised the money to pay the workers.

One evening Mrs. Bethune walked to the site upon which she would build her school. It was still piled high with rubbish. She just stood there with a smile on her face. A passerby stopped and asked, "What do you see in that junk that makes you smile?"

"Why, it's my school. Don't you see it?"

The man stood looking at the old junk heap. "You know," he said after a while, "I believe I do." Mrs. Bethune had that rare ability to pull people into her dreams.

The School, as it was called, limped along. Mrs. Bethune wore many hats—teacher, administrator, fund-raiser, and

"Mother Dear" to her girls. But in order to grow she needed help. She couldn't make it on the small donations. Tuition was not adequate, but she didn't want to raise it. What she needed was a patron, a wealthy person who would invest in the future of young black girls. There were plenty of millionaires in Daytona; she decided to present her case to as many as would listen.

Within the next few months, Mrs. Bethune found not one, but several patrons who would remain friends to her school throughout their lives. The list was impressive. It included oil magnate John D. Rockefeller and industrialist Henry J. Kaiser. But it was James G. Gamble of Procter and Gamble who would become a lifelong benefactor and devoted friend to Mrs. Bethune.

Mr. Gamble received a letter from Mrs. Bethune telling him about her school for black children. She didn't ask for money, only an opportunity to discuss her plans. He agreed to a meeting. Mr. Gamble was so impressed he asked if he might visit the following day.

"This is a new kind of school," Mrs. Bethune explained. "I am teaching girls crafts and homemaking as well as reading and writing. I am teaching them to earn a living."

Mrs. Bethune showed Mr. Gamble the lot she was buying and the school she planned to build there. Then she asked if he would serve on the first board of trustees. "I want the board to be integrated," she said.

Mr. Gamble smiled. "This is the first time I've ever been asked to be the trustee of a dream. I hope I am worthy."

Before he left that day, Mr. Gamble left a sizable donation and agreed to help Mrs. Bethune in any way he could. He never failed on that promise.

Not all people thought Mrs. Bethune's work was worthy of praise. To some she was a troublemaker, filling blacks with ideas that made them "forget their place." Others felt she was not giving black girls a proper education. She was accused of training her girls to be servants.

In the early twentieth century, black educators had polarized into two opposing sides. One side—led by W.E.B. DuBois, a Harvard graduate—argued that blacks needed to be trained as doctors, lawyers, businessmen, and social workers in order to fight injustice and build a strong economic base in the black community. DuBois believed that, given the opportunity, blacks could build their own corporations and businesses. Another side argued that it made no sense to be a lawyer when no court in the land allowed a black man to present a case. There were very few jobs for black professionals. This side, led by Booker T. Washington, advocated teaching blacks skills such as bricklaying, carpentry, and animal husbandry. Both sides made valid points.

But while they argued, Mary Bethune was doing the best she could with what she had. Her students were given a sound academic curriculum—reading, writing, and math. At the same time, she included homemaking classes such as cooking and sewing. With these skills the girls could always get jobs. If they had higher goals of college, she saw to it that they were prepared to go on. "There is no such thing as menial labor, only menial self-esteem," she used to say. She taught her girls to glorify *any* job they did by doing it well.

Still, that did not stop some poeple from denouncing her and her school. Once she was a visitor in a church where the preacher said, "I'd rather see my daughter go to hell and be taught by Satan himself than by Mary McLeod Bethune." Mrs. Bethune never lost her composure. After the service, the pastor asked her who she was. "I am Mary McLeod Bethune," she said. "I thoroughly enjoyed your service." But she was hurt much more than she ever let on.

For years she had trained herself to meet anger with kindness, bigotry with dignity, hatred with love. But one day she lost all control. Those who heard Mrs. Bethune tell the story later say that she embellished it generously with hand gestures and voice inflections.

Here is what happened. Hotels were springing up overnight in Daytona. As each new hotel opened, Mrs. Bethune approached the owner to arrange musical concerts.

Most of the hotel owners welcomed her and made arrangements for her choir to entertain their guests. As much as $150 could be raised in one evening. The Oak Hotel had just opened, and Mrs. Bethune climbed the front steps and knocked on the door. The owner, an elderly white woman, ordered her around to the back door. Mrs. Bethune began to explain why she was there, but the woman interrupted her with, "Nigger, get off here, or I will throw you off!"

Mrs. Bethune had called on her reservoir of calm too many times. This time the anger was unleashed. Mrs. Bethune pulled herself taller. Then with clenched fists on her hips, she snapped back, "You can say what you want to, but don't you touch me or somebody will have to come pick *you* up off *your* front porch!" Mrs. Bethune spat as she walked away.

Whenever Mrs. Bethune told this story, there was never remorse in her voice, no hint of an apology. It seemed she almost enjoyed it. However, she was careful not to let outbursts like that happen often.

With the help of Mr. Gamble, the board of trustees was formed and plans for the new school were underway. Although the building wasn't finished, the school was moved from the house on Oak Street to the new Faith Hall in 1906, the same year Samuel died.

Chapter 8

MARY McLEOD BETHUNE, THE CRUSADER

Mrs. Bethune was called Mary by her closest friends, but all others were required to preface her name with "Mrs.," a term southern whites rarely used when addressing black women.

Her reputation for being the "cleanest woman on earth" earned her the well-deserved title of "the dirt chaser." One day while she was whitewashing the front steps of Faith Hall, two men passed. "Be careful," one man said to the other, "or she'll whitewash you." Even when walking along the street, Mrs. Bethune would stoop to pull a weed or pick up a piece of trash. Daily cleaning and personal hygiene were requirements at her school.

To all her students, Mrs. Bethune was "Mother Dear," a name she preferred over all the other titles she held. The name reflected the close relationship that existed between Mrs. Bethune and her students. Like a mother, Mrs. Bethune worried about her girls. When they were happy, she was happy. When one of them hurt, she hurt. That's why when Anita Pinkey didn't show up for class, Mrs. Bethune became worried.

Mrs. Bethune hurried to Anita's room. The girl's head was burning with fever; she was doubled over in pain. Even an untrained eye could see that the child was suffering from acute appendicitis. Mrs. Bethune bundled Anita in a blanket and rushed her to the nearest hospital.

"You know we don't take colored here," said the nurse. At times like these Mrs. Bethune didn't waste time arguing with "the help." She asked to see the doctor in charge, Dr. C.C. Bahannon. "Sorry, but that's just the way it is," he said.

It was only after Mrs. Bethune reminded him of the physician's oath that he agreed to perform the surgery. Exhausted from the ordeal, Mrs. Bethune went back to the school to let the other girls know Anita was going to be all right.

But the next day when Mother Bethune went to see "her child," she found Anita on the back porch behind the kitchen. How could a person be expected to recover from major surgery on a back porch! "No human being should have to endure such a thing," she said angrily.

In 1911, there was no black hospital in Daytona, but there was one black physician, Dr. T.A. Adams. He was not permitted to perform surgery or admit his patients at any of the private white hospitals. Mrs. Bethune went to see him. When they parted he was the director of the McLeod Hospital. The trouble was that the hospital only existed in Mrs. Bethune's mind. By the end of that year, however, "Colored Town" had a hospital.

Next to Faith Hall was a small cottage. Mrs. Bethune bought it and, with Dr. Adams's help, opened a small two-bed hospital. Within the next few years the cottage was replaced by a new two-story building with twenty-six beds. McLeod Hospital served the black community in Daytona and surrounding areas from 1911 to 1939, when it was made a part of the city hospital system. Then, the old hospital building was converted into the Keyser Laboratory, a practice school for teacher training.

By 1912, Mary's first students had completed eighth grade and were taking high school classes, although the school had not been accredited. In order to be accredited, Mrs. Bethune knew she needed a solid curriculum and a strong faculty. Mrs. Frances R. Keyser, a graduate of Hunter College in New York, was one of the earliest faculty members she hired. "I need strong women to help me realize this vision," Mrs. Bethune told her. "And the best offer I can make now is thirty dollars a month."

Mrs. Keyser's response was, "If I receive only thirty cents, I will come." By building a talented, well-qualified, and dedicated staff, Mrs. Bethune's school became an accredited high school and two-year college. It had the only black library in the area, and held adult education classes.

Then in 1914 Mr. Thomas H. White, president of White Sewing Machine Company, a board member and a good friend of Mrs. Bethune's, suddenly died. For years Mr. White had been one of the school's most faithful supporters. His death was deeply felt.

It was Mr. White who had donated the money to complete Faith Hall. It was he who had given Mrs. Bethune the money to buy the cottage that became McLeod Hospital. Using his power, he had persuaded the city of Daytona to extend water and electric services to the school. And he had bought the land that was to become the school farm called "The Retreat."

He had been so generous that, after he had bought the land for the farm, Mrs. Bethune felt she couldn't ask him for one more penny. But, for the farm to be productive she needed a mule, and there was no money to buy one. Mrs. Bethune approached Mr. White in this manner:

"I need your advice," she said.

"Nothing easier to give," he answered.

"Do you know much about mules?"

"Not much. A bit out of my line."

Then Mrs. Bethune explained that the farm needed a mule, but she hated to spend the money unless it was a good mule, worth the money. The next day, Mr. White returned with the animal in tow. "You picked a good animal. Well worth the price," he said.

Mrs. Bethune named the mule "Old Bush" because he had a bushy tail like the one she had ridden as a child. Old Bush made it possible for The Retreat to be a working farm that brought in revenue for the school.

Mr. White would be missed, but never forgotten. In his will he left the school $79,000. Two years later when the new administration building was opened, it was appropriately named White Hall.

Mrs. Bethune was becoming nationally recognized as a leader, and she was invited to join many organizations. The Urban League, started in 1910 by New York social workers to improve black American life, asked her to become a board member. She accepted the position with great pride. The National Association for the Advancement of Colored People (NAACP) was founded in 1909, six years before the Ku Klux Klan (KKK) was formed on Stone Mountain in Georgia. Mrs. Bethune was familiar with the work of both organizations. The NAACP fought for the rights of black Americans in the nation's courts; the Klan burned homes and terrorized blacks under the cloak of darkness and white sheets.

Mrs. Bethune worked with the NAACP, and in so doing became a target of the Klan. Once, when she was out of town, the Klan marched in front of Faith Hall. The teachers were frightened, but the younger children thought it was a Halloween march and laughed at the hooded klansmen who paraded past with burning crosses. The Klan was no laughing matter; but Mrs. Bethune had friends in powerful places, and so the march was held only to serve as a "warning."

When she returned Mrs. Bethune denounced Klan activities and challenged them to face her in the daylight without their protective hoods. No one ever did. The harassment soon ended.

During World War I, Mrs. Bethune was placed in charge of the local Florida chapter of the Red Cross in West Palm Beach. The National Association of Colored Women elected her their president. During their convention in California in 1915, Mrs. Bethune delivered a moving speech to the organization, calling on each member to work toward improving the lives of black American women. She received a standing ovation.

Sitting on stage that day was an elderly white woman. A bouquet of flowers was brought to the stage. Mrs. Bethune turned to present them to the guest of honor, Mrs. Mary Crissman, the woman who had made it possible for her to attend Scotia and Moody. It was a touching moment for both of them, since they had never met in person. When they embraced, there was not a dry eye in the audience. Then tearfully, Mrs. Bethune made one last plea: "Invest in a human soul," she said, " . . . it might be a diamond in the rough." No doubt Mrs. Bethune was thinking about her own life.

Mary Bethune in one of her many visits to the White House

Chapter 9

MARY McLEOD BETHUNE,
THE COLLEGE PRESIDENT

Mrs. Bethune spoke before numerous organizations, pleading for help for her school. She told stories to illustrate how the school had survived.

A story the audiences seemed to enjoy most was about a wealthy widow named Mrs. Curtis. For years Mrs. Bethune kept a record of every penny donated to the school. She logged the contributor's name, the date, and the amount received. In addition, she sent the person copies of *The Advocate*, the school newspaper.

There was a woman named Flora B. Curtis who came to the school to purchase a small amount of vegetables every week. She always fussed over the carrots and peas and complained about the quality. "You can't ask top price for inferior goods," she said as she begrudgingly paid for the vegetables. Mrs. Bethune instructed her students to stay patient.

The students who had to deal with Mrs. Curtis wondered if the few cents she spent each week were worth the aggravation.

Mrs. Bethune logged every penny Mrs. Curtis spent, and added her name to *The Advocate*'s mailing list.

Then one winter day, Mrs. Curtis appeared at Mrs. Bethune's study door. Inviting her in, Mrs. Bethune noticed how frail her visitor appeared. Mrs. Curtis took a seat. "I've been buying vegetables from your school for some time now," she said.

"Yes, you have," answered Mrs. Bethune, taking out her account book. Within a few minutes Mrs. Bethune had totaled the entire amount Mrs. Curtis had spent over the years—about $20.

"Your students have always been so kind to me," said Mrs. Curtis. "I am very particular, you know. Oh, and I want to thank you for sending me the school newspaper," she added. "I look forward to each issue."

Mrs. Bethune helped her visitor to the door. They never met again. Mrs. Curtis died shortly afterwards, having willed $80,000 to the school! When the new dormitory opened in 1922, it was named Curtis Hall.

There is a similar story that audiences always enjoyed. Mrs. Bethune graciously accepted a twenty-five-cent donation from S.J. Peabody, the well-known philanthropist. But at that time he was not well known; the name meant nothing to Mrs. Bethune. He was simply another person who had given. She dutifully noted the name, date, and amount of the donation.

A while later Mr. Peabody returned. "I was here some time ago," he said. "I believe I gave a donation." Mrs. Bethune took out her account book. After verifying the date of his visit, she added. "Yes, you were here in March. You gave us twenty-five cents." Mr. Peabody was impressed. Before leaving he wrote a check for $250 and gave her the money to equip the auditorium in White Hall.

Mary McLeod Bethune knew that she had at last crossed the river. The school was going to survive. But it couldn't grow unless she had more consistent financial support.

One hundred miles away in Jacksonville, Florida, Cookman College—run by the Methodist Episcopal Church North—had stopped growing. Enrollment was down, faculty turnover was high, and student morale low. The school had money, but it was dying.

The Methodist board of education knew that Mrs. Bethune had an excellent faculty at Daytona, and that the school had experienced steady growth for almost twenty years. Cookman had been founded in 1872 by Reverend D.B.S. Darnell under the Board of Missions for Freedmen of the Presbyterian Church in the United States. In 1923, Mrs. Bethune and the officials at Cookman began discussing a merger of the two schools. By 1925 the plans were completed and the school became known as Bethune-Cookman College.

To gain something, Mrs. Bethune had had to give something. For financial stability, she relinquished her total control. Under the terms of the agreement the school became coeducational. All financial planning was handled by the Methodist Educational Board, and Mrs. Bethune remained the school's president.

On the day the legal papers were signed, Mrs. Bethune made this statement:

> It is a big thing to yield all. My feet are sore now, my limbs are tired, my mind weary. I have gone over hills and valleys, everywhere begging for nickels and dimes that have paid for this soil, these buildings, for this equipment that you find here. . . . In yielding my power, my personal power, my mental power, I am doing it with the confidence that you will never fail me. . . .

Her trust was not betrayed. Bethune-Cookman College

still stands as a living, ever-expanding monument to the woman who started it with $1.50.

After the merger, the Methodist church became responsible for administering the school's finances. Mrs. Bethune could no longer call it "her" school exclusively, but she ran it the same way she always had. As the college's president, Mrs. Bethune was busier than ever. But she loved every minute of it.

"When is the last time you had a vacation?" one of her friends asked. Mrs. Bethune couldn't answer. For over twenty years she had worked night and day for the school that carried her name. Now that its future was secure, she could think of herself. In 1927 Mary McLeod Bethune went to Europe.

The trip was a real adventure that took in the major European capitals. Mrs. Bethune charmed British gentry, and was often mistaken for royalty herself. Whenever the opportunity presented itself she talked about Bethune-Cookman and the work being done there.

One of the trip's highlights came when Lady Edith McLeod invited Mrs. Bethune to tea. Lady McLeod's ancestors had owned Mary's ancestors. What might have been a tense meeting turned into a mutually enjoyable afternoon. Mrs. Bethune couldn't help but think, "Wouldn't Samuel love the

idea that his daughter was sipping tea with Lady McLeod?"
She said later, "The tea was the best I've ever tasted."

One thing Mrs. Bethune noticed was the lack of racial discrimination in Europe. Racism didn't raise its ugly head until one evening when her party went to a restaurant in London. An American protested to the owner that he was not accustomed to eating with Negroes. The owner graciously bowed, but added, "I don't know what the custom is in the United States, but here the customer receives what he pays for."

On to Paris. With childlike enthusiasm, Mrs. Bethune took in the sights of the French captial. Since her days at Scotia she had been interested in art; she visited museum after museum. What a thrill to see the "real" paintings. Mrs. Bethune loved Italy and Germany. The people loved her too. Mary McLeod Bethune was rapidly becoming the toast of the continent that season. Invitations poured in; she even received two serious proposals of marriage, which she graciously refused. "I have a school to run," she said. "I can't give that up."

It was in Switzerland that Mrs. Bethune saw something she had no idea existed. The gardeners in Switzerland had developed a black rose. When she knelt in the dirt and carefully touched its soft petals, she wept tears of joy.

Once, when she was a student at Moody, she had visited a white home. The child thought Mary was dirty and needed to "wash the black from her hands and face." Gently Mary had explained to the child that the color didn't wash off. A vase of flowers sat nearby. "God is like a gardener. His world is a garden," she said to the child. "People are like flowers. Each one is different, but each one just as beautiful to the Gardener."

Mrs. Bethune used the story often to illustrate equality, but there was no known black flower to make the point more vivid. To her knowledge no such flower existed. There in Switzerland she found the answer. Mrs. Bethune ordered a dozen plants to be shipped to Bethune-Cookman.

The world "flower garden" was her favorite analogy, and the black rose became her trademark.

All too soon, it was time to go home. When she returned to the college, she was refreshed. "I would not change whatever I am for any other that I have seen," she said.

It was good Mrs. Bethune took the trip. Hard times were ahead.

Mary Bethune welcomes Eleanor Roosevelt to Bethune-Cookman College. The two women had many interests in common and liked and respected one another.

Chapter 10

MARY McLEOD BETHUNE, THE PRESIDENTIAL ADVISER

In 1928, one-hundred-mile-an-hour winds swept over the coast of Florida, leaving hundreds dead and millions of dollars worth of property damaged. Mrs. Bethune rushed to the scene and worked long, hard hours with the Red Cross. "Never in my life had I seen such suffering." She wanted to stay longer, but word came that her school was in trouble.

When she was sure the immediate crisis was under control, Mrs. Bethune went home. Ten thousand loads of sand were needed to refill the washed-away land at a cost of a dollar a load. "Begin delivery," she said to the contractor. Where was the money coming from? Within three days, she had the full $10,000 in cash. Once again, Mary McLeod Bethune had found a way to keep the school running.

The 1928 hurricane paled in comparison to the "Crash of 1929." The stock market fell to an all-time low, marking the beginning of the Great Depression. While the country teeter-tottered on the brink of total disaster, Mrs. Bethune tried to keep a level head. First, she discontinued her own salary, cut staff salaries, but flatly refused to cut back any programs. "We will survive this," she said. "But we must not be led by panic." She was not as confident as it appeared on the surface. The light in her study burned long into the night as she pondered over figures, trying to "make a way." She bolstered her courage with prayer, and met each day as it came with an almost childlike faith that things would get better.

In 1932 the Democratic candidate, Franklin Delano Roosevelt, was elected president of the United States. Roosevelt began introducing programs to offset the effects of the Depression. One of these programs was the National Youth Administration, directed by Aubrey Williams. The purpose of the NYA was to give part-time employment to students so they could continue their education and to train and employ idle young people who were not in school.

Word came to Mrs. Bethune that the president had appointed her to the advisory committee of the newly formed NYA. She accepted the post and went to Washington. It was the beginning of an era later to be known as the New Deal. It was also the beginning of a new chapter in the life of a woman who had dedicated her life to youth.

When Mrs. Bethune and President Roosevelt met—after she had been with the NYA about a year—she left an indelible impression on him.

"In many parts of the South," she told Roosevelt in her slow, deliberate voice, "the $15 or $20 check each month means real salvation for thousands of Negro young people. We are bringing life and spirit to these many thousands who for so long have been in darkness. I speak, Mr. President, not as Mrs. Bethune but as the voice of fourteen million Americans who seek to achieve full citizenship. We want to continue to open doors for these millions."

The president wept when she finished. He grasped her hand. "Mrs. Bethune," he said, "I am glad I am able to contribute something to help make a better life for your people."

For her work on behalf of black youth, Mrs. Bethune was awarded the NAACP Spingarn Medal in 1935. This award was, and still is, given for "the highest or noblest achievement by an American Negro during the preceding year or years." Other winners before her included George Washington Carver, the scientist; James Weldon Johnson, the poet; W.E.B. DuBois, a founder of the NAACP and the Pan-African Congress; and Carter Woodson, historian. Later

Mrs. Bethune worked with Woodson to write an accurate history of black Americans.

In accepting the award she wrote to Walter White, secretary of the NAACP,

> Your letter has completely overwhelmed me. ... This year has been such a hard one and we are just going into the last month of it. It is so significant my burdens are thus lightened by this recognition. . . . I never feel worthy of honors, but they are great stimuli to my strength and faith and courage.

President Roosevelt formed the Office of Minority Affairs, a branch of the NYA, and Mrs. Bethune was appointed as its administrator. This was a full-time job that would require her to live in Washington. It was a tough decision to make.

"I have to take care of my college," she protested, not realizing that a job had never been created for a black woman in any previous administration. It was a first in American government. But she could not accept.

The president said simply, "I'm afraid you'll have to."

Mrs. Bethune moved to Washington and left her beloved college in the capable hands of her staff.

For the first time in over thirty years, Mary McLeod

Bethune had a steady paycheck. She sent well over half of it to the school to help defer expenses. Mrs. Bethune was not a nine-to-five worker; she was the first to arrive in the morning and sometimes she was still there when workers returned the following morning. Under her direction, over six thousand black youths had jobs in building projects, road repair, and forest conservation. "Not alms but opportunity," she said as she continued to speak to groups across the country.

Congress threatened to cut the $100,000 graduate-training fund from the budget. Bursting into the president's office, she protested, "Think what a terrible tragedy it would be for America if, by this action by a committee of Congress, Negroes would be deprived of the leadership of skilled and trained members of their race!"

Realizing she had interrupted the president of the United States, she quickly composed herself and apologized. President Roosevelt smiled. "My heart is with you," he said. The next week Congress approved the funding.

During her years with the NYA Mrs. Bethune called on the president many times. He always greeted her cheerfully. "It's so good to see you, Mrs. Bethune."

"I don't know why," she answered. "I'm always asking for something."

"Yes," said the president, "but you never ask for yourself."

Mrs. Bethune was also a frequent visitor to the White House, and she and the president's wife, Eleanor Roosevelt, formed a lasting friendship that superceded politics. They both shared an interest in the rights of women and youth. There were a few white visitors who attended White House functions who didn't know how to handle being in the company of a black woman. Mrs. Bethune and Mrs. Roosevelt secretly enjoyed making bigots uncomfortable.

Mary McLeod Bethune gave the impression that she was invincible, but age was taking its toll. She was, in fact, quite human. In 1940 she was admitted to Johns Hopkins Hospital in Baltimore to undergo nasal surgery to relieve an asthmatic condition. She was the first black person to be admitted to Johns Hopkins. Nobody dared turn her away, but a private room was prepared for her so white patients would not be "offended." Mrs. Bethune had power and she knew how to use it—the same way she had gotten Samuel a fair price at the cotton market—with tact. There were no black doctors on staff. She knew it. "I'd like to have a black doctor assist with my surgery," she said, rather matter-of-factly. After that there were black doctors at Johns Hopkins.

When a young nurse insisted on calling her "Mary," she countered, "Do I know you? Are we personal friends?" That was enough. The nurse apologized, and the two women became friends.

Hitler's army was on the move. War was inevitable. But it was the surprise attack on Pearl Harbor, December 7, 1941, that pulled the United States into World War II. In 1942, the NYA was temporarily closed. Mrs. Bethune resigned as president of Bethune-Cookman College which, by then, was on solid financial footing. Professor James A. Colston became its new president. Against her doctor's advice, and at the age of sixty-five, she accepted the position of special assistant to the Secretary of War to aid in the selection of Negro officer candidates in the Women's Army Corps (WAC).

Mrs. Bethune was in Dallas when word came that the president had died at his home in Warm Springs, Georgia. The Roosevelt years had come to an end. It was the end of an era, but not the end for Mary McLeod Bethune.

Chapter 11

MARY McLEOD BETHUNE, A GREAT AMERICAN

President Roosevelt was dead, but his spirit lived on. Plans he had made to hold the San Francisco Conference on April 25, 1945, continued. The purpose of the conference was to write the charter for the United Nations—a charter that would guarantee freedom and democracy to all people of the world.

At Mrs. Roosevelt's insistence, Mrs. Bethune was named as a consultant along with Walter White and W.E.B. DuBois, the only other blacks in attendence. For Mrs. Bethune it was the crowning of an incredible life. From a cotton picker to a world leader—that in itself was remarkable.

She was not well, but during her five-week stay in San Francisco she spoke to thousands of college students. She encouraged them to strive for excellence, work for peace and brotherhood, and never lose faith.

The climax of her work at the conference was a statement

written jointly with Mr. White and Dr. DuBois:

> It is our hope as consultants to the American delegation to induce the San Francisco Conference to face what is one of the most serious problems of the twentieth century—the question of race and color. We are particularly concerned with what is done about colonial empires and the well-being of peoples of color. What happens to even the most exploited of these has direct bearing upon the future of Negroes in the United States.

Although Mr. Roosevelt didn't live to see his dream fulfilled, the United Nations came into being. Mrs. Bethune lived to see the General Assembly issue its universal Declaration of Human Rights. If Patsy McLeod had been alive she might have declared, "Our day of deliverance has come!"

Mrs. Bethune's health was failing, but she stubbornly refused to stop, although she did slow down a little. In her late seventies she traveled to Haiti, then returned to Mayesville. The old Homestead was gone—burned down long ago. Miss Wilson's school suffered from woeful neglect. It was 1950. Amazing how little had changed. She shook her head and walked away.

At last she settled down at The Retreat, her home on Bethune-Cookman's campus farm. There she enjoyed the fruits of her labor. Students came daily to see to her needs. Countless nieces and nephews showered her with love and affection, and carefully dusted her collection of glass, wooden, porcelain, ivory, and crystal elephants. Bert had married and was a grandfather himself. Then on May 18, 1955, Mary McLeod Bethune died of a heart attack. The world mourned. Her body was buried on the grounds of The Retreat, her gravestone simply marked "Mother."

In her will she wrote:

Sometimes I ask myself if I have any legacy to leave. My worldly possessions are few. Yet, my experiences have been rich. From them I distilled principles and policies in which I firmly believe. Perhaps, in them, there is something of value, so, as my life draws to a close, I will pass them on. . . . Here, then, is my legacy: I leave you LOVE; I leave you HOPE; I leave you a THIRST FOR EDUCATION; I leave you FAITH; I leave you RACIAL DIGNITY; I leave you A DESIRE TO LIVE HARMON-IOUSLY WITH YOUR FELLOW MEN; I

leave you, finally, A RESPONSIBILITY TO
OUR YOUNG PEOPLE.

Epilogue

The founder of the school built on a junk heap would be proud of the living, growing institution that bears her name. Bethune-Cookman College is a monument to a woman and her work.

The little girl who sang on her way to Miss Wilson's school would be proud of the internationally-recognized Bethune-Cookman choir. The frightened young girl who was awed by the magnificent Graves Hall at Scotia would be happy to see the well-kept, forty-four-acre campus surrounded by trees and beautiful flowers.

The teacher whose first students had to sleep crosswise in bed would nod her approval at the college's six dormitories that house over a thousand regular students. She would be proud of the B.A. and B.S. degrees that are awarded to those candidates who complete the required work in English, business, fine and performing arts, math and science, philosophy, social work, and engineering.

It would give her great satisfaction to know that 80 percent of the freshmen who enter Bethune-Cookman graduate.

The woman who was affectionately called "Mother" would be delighted to know that graduates of Bethune-Cookman hold managerial positions in government, business, journalism, the military, the visual and performing arts, and sports. All this would please Mary McLeod Bethune, but it wouldn't surprise her.

Whenever her students performed well, Mrs. Bethune would throw back her head and clap her hands joyfully. "Look at my children," she'd say. "Aren't they beautiful? I knew they could do it!"

With encouragement like that, who can fail? The legacy she left Bethune-Cookman College was what her father had given her at birth—hope. "With faith," she often said, "you can make it."

Mary McLeod Bethune 1875-1955

1875 Mary McLeod is born in Mayesville, South Carolina. A Civil Rights Act gives blacks equal rights in public places, though school integration is not included; Supreme Court declares the act invalid in 1883. Revenue officials known as the Whiskey Ring are indicted for conspiracy to defraud the government of whiskey revenues. Samuel Lowery starts a school for blacks in Huntsville, Alabama. Rebellion begins in Cuba.

1876 Winner of U.S. presidential election is in dispute. Sitting Bull massacres Custer's troops at Little Big Horn. Secretary of War William Belknap is impeached for taking bribes for the sale of trading posts in Indian Territory. Alexander Graham Bell patents the telephone. Mark Twain publishes *The Adventures of Tom Sawyer*.

1877 U.S. presidential electoral commission rules that Rutherford B. Hayes won the 1876 elections. Reconstruction of the South ends. Russia and Serbia declare war on Turkey; Russia invades Rumania and other areas.

1878 Thomas Edison invents the incandescent electric lamp. Turkey-Russia armistice is signed.

1879 Large numbers of blacks begin migrating from the South, mainly to the Midwest. Construction of the Panama Canal begins.

1880 James Garfield is elected president. France annexes Tahiti. Transvaal declares itself a republic, independent of Britain. Joel Chandler Harris publishes *Uncle Remus* stories.

1881 President Garfield is assassinated; Vice-president Chester A. Arthur becomes president. First "Jim Crow" law is passed in Tennessee to segregate railroad coaches. Tuskegee Institute, with Booker T. Washington as head, is founded. Tsar Alexander II of Russia is assassinated.

1882 New York City installs first electric street lamps. U.S. bans Chinese immigration for the next ten years.

1883 As a result of five Supreme Court civil rights cases, the 1875 Civil Rights Act is declared invalid; Court said the act protected social, not political, rights; further ruled that states may not invade a person's civil rights, but that individuals, unaided by the state, may do so. World's first skyscraper, ten stories high, is built in Chicago. New York's Brooklyn Bridge is opened.

1884 Mary McLeod enters Miss Emma Wilson's school. France presents the Statue of Liberty to the U.S. Grover Cleveland is elected president.

1885 Civil War Union General Ulysses S. Grant dies. Louis Pasteur develops a rabies vaccine.

1886 Anarchists riot in Chicago's Haymarket Square. American Federation of Labor is founded. Bonaparte and Orleans families are expelled from France.

1887 Mary McLeod enters Scotia Seminary in Concord, North Carolina. Interstate Commerce Commission, first regulatory commission in U.S., is established.

1888 Benjamin Harrison is elected president. Kaiser Wilhelm II becomes emperor of Germany. "Jack the Ripper" murders six London women.

1889 Barnum and Bailey's Circus opens in London. Austrian Crown Prince Archduke Rudolph commits suicide.

1890 Daughters of the American Revolution (DAR) is founded in Washington, D.C. Japan holds its first general elections. Influenza epidemics flare up around the world.

1891 Famine sweeps Russia. Earthquake in Japan kills 10,000 people. Dutch anthropologist Eugene Dubois discovers prehistoric Java Man.

1892 Grover Cleveland is elected president. Lynching of blacks rises to 160 incidents this year (1,400 since 1882). Iron and steel workers go on strike.

1893 Henry Ford constructs his first automobile. World's Columbian Exhibition opens in Chicago.

1894 Mary McLeod graduates from Scotia Seminary and enters Moody Bible College in Chicago. Korea and Japan declare war on China. Hawaii becomes a republic, following a *coup d'etat*.

1895 Booker T. Washington introduces his race relations program, the "Atlanta Compromise," in Alabama. Cuba begins fighting Spain for independence. Chinese are defeated in war with Japan.

1896 "Separate but equal" railroad accommodations are upheld by Supreme Court in *Plessy v. Ferguson* case. William McKinley is elected president. Klondike Gold Rush begins in Alaska. Mary Church Terrell helps found the National Association of Colored Women. Harriet Beecher Stowe, author of *Uncle Tom's Cabin*, dies.

1897 First U.S. subway line opens in Boston. Severe famine hits India. Slavery is abolished in Zanzibar.

1898 Mary McLeod and Albertus Bethune are married in Sumter, South Carolina. Literacy tests and poll taxes as voting requirements are upheld in *Williams v. Mississippi* lawsuit. Spanish-American War begins, and ends in Treaty of Paris; U.S. acquires the Philippines, Puerto Rico, and Guam; Cuba gains independence from Spain.

1899 Albert McLeod Bethune is born. Mary McLeod Bethune moves to Palatka, Florida. Boer War begins in South Africa.

1900 William McKinley is reelected president. Bubonic plague epidemic breaks out in the U.S. 231 foreign civilians are killed in China's Boxer Rebellion.

1901 President William McKinley is assassinated; Theodore Roosevelt becomes president. England's Queen Victoria dies at 81 after reigning 64 years. First Nobel Prizes are awarded, from a fund given by Alfred Nobel, inventor of dynamite. Boers in South Africa begin guerrilla warfare.

1902 U.S. coal workers go on strike. Cuba becomes an independent republic. South Africa Boer War ends.

1903 Mary McLeod Bethune moves to Daytona, Florida. Orville and Wilbur Wright fly the first airplane at Kitty Hawk, North Carolina. Settlement of Alaskan frontier begins.

1904 Mary McLeod Bethune opens Daytona Educational and Industrial School for Negro Girls in Daytona, Florida. Theodore Roosevelt is elected to a second presidential term. Russia declares war on Japan. Paris Conference meets to discuss white slave trade.

1905 W.E.B. DuBois's Niagara Conference calls for equal rights, opportunities, education, and justice. Russian troops massacre workers in St. Petersburg on "Bloody Sunday." Russo-Japanese war ends in Treaty of Portsmouth.

1906 Samuel McLeod (Mary's father) dies. Mary McLeod Bethune moves her school to Faith Hall in

104

Daytona, Florida. Brownsville Affair results in dishonorable discharge of 167 black soldiers for alleged misconduct in Brownsville, Texas; guilt is lifted in 1972. First radio broadcast of a voice and music program takes place. Upton Sinclair's exposé of Chicago stockyard conditions, *The Jungle*, leads to U.S. Pure Food and Drug Act.

1907 President Roosevelt bars Japanese immigration. First electric washing machine is invented in Chicago.

1908 William Howard Taft is elected president. Jack Johnson is first black world heavyweight boxing champion. Ford Motor Company manufactures the first Model "T" car.

1909 National Association for the Advancement of Colored People (NAACP) is founded to improve blacks' job opportunities and police protection. Explorer Robert E. Peary reaches the North Pole.

1910 National Urban League is formed to help blacks adjust economically and socially to city life. Marcus Garvey's Universal Negro Improvement Association adopts bill of rights and proposes blacks' emigration to Africa. China abolishes slavery.

1911 McLeod Hospital opens in Daytona, Florida. Chinese Revolution begins; Manchu dynasty falls; Chinese Republic is proclaimed, with Sun Yat-sen as president. Explorer Roald Amundsen reaches the South Pole.

1912 Woodrow Wilson is elected president. The *Titanic* crashes into an iceberg and sinks on its first voyage.

1913 Mahatma Gandhi is arrested in India for leading passive resistance movement. Balkan wars begin.

1914 Garrilo Princip assassinates Archduke Francis Ferdinand in Sarajevo, Yugoslavia; World War I Begins. Panama Canal opens. Black musician W.C. Handy composes "Saint Louis Blues."

1915 World War I continues: Germans sink the *Lusitania*. Albert Einstein introduces his general theory of relativity. Alexander Graham Bell and Thomas Watson hold the first transcontinental telephone conversation.

1916 Woodrow Wilson is reelected president. World War I continues.

1917 U.S. declares war on Germany and enters World War I. Bolshevik revolution begins in St. Petersburg. First jazz phonograph recordings are made. Four women are arrested for picketing White House for women's voting rights.

1918 World War I ends. Austria, Hungary, Bavaria, and Germany become republics. Air Mail service and daylight saving time begin in U.S.

1919 Eighteenth Amendment passes, prohibiting sale of alcoholic beverages. Race riots break out in Chicago. First League of Nations meeting is held in Paris.

1920 Warren G. Harding is elected president. Nineteenth Amendment gives women the right to vote. Marcus Garvey opens National Convention of Universal Negro Improvement Association. Black cultural movement, Harlem Renaissance, is underway and continues for a decade. Ku Klux Klan revival begins.

1921 U.S. limits integration with Quota Act. U.S. signs postwar treaties with Germany, Austria, and Hungary. Paris conference of Allies sets German war debts at $33 billion. The "Unknown Soldier" is buried at Arlington National Cemetery. Ku Klux Klan activities become increasingly violent.

1922 Union of Soviet Socialist Republics is formed. Benito Mussolini gains dictatorial powers in Italy. Mahatma Gandhi is imprisoned for civil disobedience in India. Ku Klux Klan gains political power.

1923 President Warren G. Harding dies; Calvin Coolidge becomes president. Hearings begin for Teapot Dome oil-lease scandal. Nazi leader Adolph Hitler is imprisoned for unsuccessful coup attempt, the "Beer Hall Putsch."

1924 Calvin Coolidge wins presidential election. J. Edgar Hoover becomes head of what is to become the Federal Bureau of Investigation. Soviet power struggle follows Nikolai Lenin's death.

1925 Bethune College and Cookman College merge to form Bethune-Cookman College. Schoolteacher John Scopes is convicted for teaching the theory of evolution, but is later acquitted. Reza Kahn becomes Shah of Iran and establishes the Pahlavi dynasty.

1926 Robert H. Goddard develops the first liquid-fuel rocket.

1927 Mary McLeod Bethune tours Europe. Supreme Court rejects Texas law against blacks voting in Democratic primary elections. Charles A. Lindbergh makes first solo airplane flight across the Atlantic. Joseph Stalin takes power in U.S.S.R. "The Jazz Singer" is the first motion picture with sound.

1928 Herbert Hoover is elected president. Congress approves $32 million to enforce Prohibition. Black newspaper *Atlanta World* is founded. Hurricane sweeps Florida coast; Mary McLeod Bethune helps in relief efforts. Amelia Earhart is first woman to fly across the Atlantic.

1929 U.S. stock market crashes, causing unemployment, worldwide depression, and business failures. In Chicago's St. Valentine's Day Massacre, members of the Moran gang are shot by rival mobsters. The term "apartheid" is first used to describe South Africa's racial policies.

1930 More than 1,300 U.S. banks close due to stock market failure. Hitler's Nazi party gains a majority in German elections. C.S. Johnson publishes *The Negro in American Civilization*.

1931 First Black Muslim Temple is established in Detroit, Michigan. Nine blacks are convicted of rape in Scottsboro, Alabama, in three famous trials; their conviction is reversed in 1935. Gangster Al Capone is imprisoned for income tax evasion.

1932 Franklin D. Roosevelt wins landslide presidential victory. Famine sweeps U.S.S.R.

1933 U.S. passes Twenty-first Amendment, repealing Prohibition. Fulgencio Batista leads a *coup d'etat* in Cuba. Adolph Hitler becomes German chancellor; democratic Weimar Republic falls; Hitler names Goebbels Minister of Propaganda. Nazis construct first concentration camp for Jews; all German political parties besides Nazi are banned.

1934 U.S.S.R. joins League of Nations. Hitler becomes president of Germany. Gandhi discontinues civil disobedience drive in India.

1935 Mary McLeod Bethune is awarded the NAACP's Spingarn Medal. Rioting in Harlem, New York leaves three dead and $200 million in property damage. Supreme Court reverses conviction of Scottsboro Nine. Germany passes anti-Jewish Nuremberg laws. Chiang Kai-chek becomes president of Chinese executive.

1936 Franklin D. Roosevelt is reelected president. Mussolini and Hitler form Rome-Berlin Axis. King Edward VIII abdicates the throne of England. Spanish Civil War begins.

1937 President Roosevelt signs U.S. Neutrality Act. George VI is crowned king of England. Japan seizes Peking, Tientsin, and Shanghai.

1938 Supreme Court rules that University of Missouri Law School must admit black students. House Committee on Un-American Activities convenes. Germany invades and annexes Austria.

1939 McLeod Hospital in Daytona, Florida becomes part of the city hospital system. Black singer Marian Anderson gives Easter concert at Lincoln Memorial in Washington, D.C., after Daughters of the American Revolution (DAR) bar her performance in Constitution Hall; first lady Eleanor Roosevelt resigns from DAR as a result. World War II begins; Germany annexes Czechoslovakia. Spanish Civil War ends; England and France recognize Franco's new government.

1940 Franklin D. Roosevelt is reelected president for a third term. Winston Churchill becomes prime minister of Great Britain. World War II continues: Germany invades Norway, Denmark, Holland, Belgium, and Luxembourg; German troops occupy Paris; Italy declares war on England and France; Germany bombs London.

1941 President Roosevelt forbids racial discrimination in government and defense industries. Supreme Court rules that railroad accommodations for blacks and whites must be equal. World War II continues: Hitler invades Russia; Japanese bomb Pearl Harbor; U.S. and Britain declare war on Japan; Germany and Italy declare war on U.S.; U.S. declares war on Germany and Italy.

1942 James Farmer founds the Congress of Racial Equality (CORE). World War II continues: Japan captures Manila and Singapore; U.S. troops land in Solomon Islands and North Africa; Battles of El Alamein (Egypt) and Solomon Islands are fought.

1943 Race riots take place in Detroit, Michigan, in Mobile, Alabama, and in Harlem, New York. Congress of Racial Equality stages a sit-in at a Chicago restaurant. World War II continues: German forces in Stalingrad surrender; Italian government collapses; Allies land in Italy; fighting in North Africa ceases.

1944 Allied forces invade Normandy and enter Paris; U.S. invades the Philippines; Battle of the Bulge begins. Supreme Court rules that blacks may vote in primary elections in the South.

1945 Franklin D. Roosevelt dies; Vice-president Harry Truman becomes president. The armed forces are desegregated. U.S. troops invade Iwo Jima and Okinawa; U.S. drops first atomic bombs on Hiroshima and Nagasaki; Hitler commits suicide; Mussolini is killed; Germany and Japan surrender; World War II ends. United Nations is founded at the San Francisco Conference.

1946 President Truman creates the Presidential Committee on Civil Rights. UN General Assembly meets for the first time, in London. Social Democrats and Communists merge in East Germany. Chinese civil war ends in a truce.

1947 President Truman recommends a civil rights section in the Department of Justice and a Fair Employment Practices Commission. Congress passes Taft-Hartley Act, controlling labor unions, over President Truman's veto.

1948 Truman wins presidential election. Segregation is prohibited by law in both armed forces and federal civil service. State of Israel is founded. Mahatma Gandhi is assassinated in India.

1949 Eleven U.S. Communists are convicted of conspiracy to overthrow the government. Apartheid policy of racial discrimination is established in South Africa. China falls to Communists; Chiang Kai-shek resigns Chinese presidency and takes his forces to Formosa (Taiwan); Mao Tse-tung proclaims People's Republic of China, with Chou En-lai as premier.

1950 Korean War begins; Douglas MacArthur commands UN forces in Korea. U.S. agrees to send arms and troops to Vietnam. Dr. Ralph J. Bunche becomes the first black to win the Nobel Peace Prize.

1951 National Guard is called to subdue riots in Cicero, Illinois, over segregated housing. Congress passes Twenty-second Amendment, setting two terms (eight years) as maximum service for president.

1952 Dwight D. Eisenhower is elected president. King George VI of England dies; his daughter becomes Queen Elizabeth II.

1953 Joseph Stalin dies; Nikita Khrushchev becomes head of Soviet Communist Party Central Committee. Marshal Tito (Joseph Broz) is elected president of Yugoslavia. Southeast Asia Treaty Organization (SEATO) is established.

1954 *Brown v. Board of Education of Topeka* Supreme Court decision reverses "separate but equal" doctrine. Senator Joseph McCarthy's anti-Communist activities accelerate, resulting in Congress's condemnation of him.

1955 Mary McLeod Bethune dies in Daytona Beach, Florida. Civil rights leader Walter White dies. President Dwight Eisenhower suffers a heart attack. Blacks' boycott of segregated buses in Montgomery, Alabama, begins.

INDEX- *Page numbers in boldface type indicate illustrations.*

Jacksonville, Florida, 83
Jennie (white friend), 18, 19
Johns Hopkins Hospital, 94
Johnson, James Weldon, 91
Johnson, Mr. (landlord), 66, 67
Kaiser, Henry J., 68
Kaiser Laboratory School, 52
Keyser, Frances R., 75, 76
Keyser Laboratory, 75
Kindrell Institute, 45
Ku Klux Klan (KKK), 77, 78
Laney, Lucy, 44
Lee, Ella, 47
Lincoln, Abraham, 12
London, England, 86
lynching, 19
Mason-Dixon Line, 12
Mayesville, South Carolina, 9, 13, 18, 22, 23, 25, 32, 38, 43, 98
McIntosh plantation, 9
McLeod, Lady Edith, 85, 86
McLeod, Hattie (sister), 44
McLeod, Mary Jane (*see* Bethune, Mary McLeod)
McLeod, Patsy (mother), 9-16, 19, 20, 23-27, 30, 33, 36, 39, 45, 47, 57, 58, 78
McLeod, Sallie (sister), 11
McLeod, Samuel (father), 9-14, 16-19, 23, 24, 26-30, 32, 36, 39, 40, 43, 45, 47, 57, 58, 72, 85, 94, 102
McLeod, William (brother), 16
McLeod Hospital, 75, 76
McLeod plantation, 9
Methodist church, 85
Methodist Educational Board, 84
Methodist Episcopal Church North, 83
Moody, Dwight L., 39
Moody Bible College, 38-40, 44, **49**, 79, 87
National Association for the Advancement of Colored People (NAACP), 77, 78, 91, 92
National Association of Colored Women, 78

National Council of Negro Women, **54, 55**
National Youth Administration (NYA), 90-93, 95
New Deal, 90
North Carolina, 30, 34, 37
Oak Hotel, Daytona, 71
Oak Street, Daytona, Florida, 63, 65, 72
Office of Minority Affairs, 92
Old Bush (mule), 15, 30, 31, 77
Palatka, Florida, 57-59
Pan-African Congress, 91
Paris, France, 86
Peabody, S.J., 83
Pinkey, Anita, 74
Presbyterian church, 35
Presbyterian Church in the United States, 84
Presbyterian Mission Board, 23, 27
Procter and Gamble, 68
racial hatred, 19
Red Cross, 78, 89
"Retreat, The" (farm), 76, 77
Retreat, The (home), 99
Roberts, Estella, 45, 46
Rockefeller, John D., 68
Roosevelt, Eleanor, **88**, 94, 97
Roosevelt, Franklin Delano, 90-95, 97, 98
San Francisco Conference, 97, 98
Satterfield, Dr. David J., 35, 37, 58
Satterfield, Mrs. David, 33-35
Savannah, Georgia, 47, 58
Scotia Seminary, 30, 31, 33-39, 44, 58, 79, 86, 101
Secretary of War, 95
sharecropping, 13, 28
Sherman, L.L., 38
Simmons, Reverend J.D., 27, 30
slavery, 9-12
Smallwood, Irene, 58
South Carolina, 9, 13, 38, 45
Spingarn Medal, 91
Stone Mountain, Georgia, 77

110

111

ABOUT THE AUTHOR

Patricia C. McKissack and her husband, Fredrick, are freelance writers, editors, and teachers of writing. They are the owners and operators of All-Writing Services, located in Clayton, Missouri. Ms. McKissack, an award-winning editor, published author, and experienced educator, has taught writing at several St. Louis colleges and universities, including Lindenwood College, the University of Missouri at St. Louis, and Forest Park Community College.

Since 1975, Ms. McKissack has published numerous magazine articles and stories for juvenile and adult readers. She has written two other biographies in the People of Distinction series, *Martin Luther King, Jr: A Man to Remember* and *Paul Laurence Dunbar: A Poet to Remember*.

Patricia McKissack is the mother of three sons. They all live in a large remodeled inner-city home in St. Louis. Aside from writing, which she considers a hobby as well as a career, Ms. McKissack likes to take care of her many plants.